Tracing The Heartlines

Every line here follows the veins of a feeling
that once lived in me.

Parul

BookLeaf
Publishing

India | USA | UK

Made with ❤ on the BookLeaf Publishing Platform
www.bookleafpub.in
www.bookleafpub.com

Dedication

To the girl who still loved and believed in love - even after the heartbreaks, even when it hurt.

Preface

I've always been someone who feels too much, the kind of person who rewatches memories until they blur, who still looks for meaning in moments that are too long gone. For the longest time, I thought love was supposed to hurt this way, that the ache meant it was real. Always choosing the love that would end up hurting me.

But somewhere between heartbreaks and healing I started writing. Not to move on, but to understand. Every poem in this book was born out of that understanding- that love isn't just about who stays, or how much pain I can endure in the name of love, it's about what stays with you when they leave.

These poems are my heartlines, each one a scar, a memory, a confession. I wrote them to remember. to forgive, and to fall back in love with myself, slowly.

If you've ever loved someone who didn't stay, or if you're learning to stay for yourself, I hope you find a piece of your own story here.
Because maybe we don't ever stop loving, we just learn to live differently with what remains.

Acknowledgements

To my mother- my constant through every storm.
Even when I fought with you, got angry, or shut you out, you stayed.
You held me when I couldn't stand, made decisions when I didn't trust myself,
and loved me when I didn't know how to love myself.

My father for always being patient through all my experimenting in life. I am blessed to be your daughter.

And to Disha (my best friend) - For listening to me until the heartbreaks didn't hurt so much anymore.
Thank you for helping me find the strength to turn it into something beautiful.

Daydreaming

In the hush of fluorescent lights,
between papers stacked and ticking time,
I am transported to castles
built out of conversations we had last night.

I imagine the electricity
when our hands would touch for the first time,
the song I'll play to tease you about your childhood
crush,
the future home with a sunlit room,
and plants in every corner
because you thought it was cool.

The stolen kisses between our meetings,
the slow mornings after late nights,
the fights about wanting more date nights,
about how you'll win me over with a pastry and a smile.

And our dog named *Hope,*
who will solve all our fights.

You will call me darling,
I will call you Sir,
in our sweet banters on rainy nights.

Our home will smell of jasmines and roses
and hum with music
while we dance till morning light

Ding...

I'm transported back into real life,
with the ache of possibilities
with my Mr. Right.
The roller-coaster of what-ifs
and traces of dreams still dancing behind my eyes.

While I'm still stuck at *hey*
and you're too busy to even reply.

*--For love stories that only lived in the head of a
hopeless romantic.*

*

....

Dhoop ki kiran sa
Choolo kabhi tum mujhe
Kabhi hawa banke
Gudguda do
Mere ishq ki milawat mei
Thoda sa rang
Apna bhi mila do

....

The first I love you

The first time you said, "I love you,"
I swear there were electrolytes in my blood,
everything rushed to my heart at once.

People say their world stops
when they hear those words;
mine began from that moment.

My heart had never felt this way before
it was new, it was terrifying.
Because deep down, I knew we were doomed to end.

So even in that rush of joy,
I cried.
Not because I doubted you,
but because I knew
your heart had chosen mine.
And I had to carry that responsibility.
Maybe only for a little while,
but I wanted to make sure
you never regretted your choice.

Its kind of impossible to know you and not love you

It's kind of impossible to know you and not love you.
To know what plays in your mind
when that song reminds you of your first heartbreak.

How your eyes turn misty
thinking about your grandma's favourite dish.
How you cry every time you visit temples.
How you sound so sure, yet still doubt yourself.

How your lips curl when you say my name.
How you make up stupid stories just to get a rise out of
me,
to check if I still love you.

How your eyes never lie.
How you're so afraid of getting hurt again
that you won't let anyone close.

How you crave company,
but can't stand the thought
of giving someone the power to hurt you again.

-from the lens of a person who tries to love the parts of me even I find hard to hold.

..

*

....

In this age of logical women,
I am the kind of girl who
thinks eye contacts
Pave path for destiny.

....

The day I realised

It was a usual conversation
past midnight, after everyone had gone to sleep.
You had work in the morning,
and I had places to be.

Somewhere between laughter and silence,
the talk drifted toward children
I told you I didn't want them
that maybe I'm too broken
to raise a child whole.

You laughed softly and said,
"But you pamper me so much, you'd
love that kid more than anyone in the world."
And I agreed,
because I wanted to believe that too.

I asked, "What do your dreams look like?"
You said you wanted a daughter
to sing her lullabies.
You hummed a few lines
and I started to cry.

You asked what happened,

and I said, "I just realised...
I'll never hear you sing it."

We stayed in silence for a while,
echoing with the noise of future
that will never see the light.

That was the night
I realised that I was in love with you.

A love that was destined to die.

-from the night I realised I was deeply in love with
someone who won't stay.

*

....

The noises in my head
take me in wild rides.

But when you hold my hand,
the storm subsides.

the noise dissolves
I feel alive.

Its serene really
how grounding you can be

All my doubts go quiet
it's just you and me.

....

Zombies pretending to be human

He walked the walk of life,
did what was expected,
chose the path less loved,
won the race,
but lost the peace.

She moved through her days
Like a well-rehearsed lullaby,
Over explaining,
Over-loving,
Being soft where it hurt.
Because that's what's expected, right?
To be the calm,
The home,
The safe place for someone else.

And oh, how they tried
Smiling at strangers,
Making everyone laugh,
Their hearts bleeding quietly
Behind perfectly covered scars.

But when the night came,

The silence was loud.
Their thoughts turned darker than the night.
They lay awake
Two zombies pretending to be human,
Scrolling through the sea of strangers.

"sleepless night?" she typed.
"It's a daily routine," he said.
"what's keeping you up?" she enquired.

For the first time in a long time,
He didn't pretend,
No masks, no sugar coating,
No pretend smile.

Two strangers on flickering screen,
Opening their hearts
Not out of trust,
But the comfort of distance,
The safety of being seen
By someone they'd never have to face.

They spoke until words
felt lighter than their feelings,
Until the ache sounded shared.
For a moment,
they were two peas in a pod,

separated by cities,
held together by confessions.

And when they finally said goodnight,
Their loneliness softened
not gone,
but gentler,
like someone had finally
understood the echo.

*-written on a night of shared misery, when they both felt
invisible, even to themselves.*

We were never meant to be

For you I was just a picture on the screen.
For me you were the muse of all my dreams.

Every monument I thought I would visit
Every cuisine I thought we would try,
For every milestone and every beach themed tattoo,
I thought your hand will be in mine.

Sometimes we would fight, but it would only be
about whose love was of better kind.

I loved expressing my love
and you liked to keep it all inside.

Let the eyes do the talking, you said.
and silences that drowned me in butterflies
And assured me of the love, you tried to hide.

You said, words would wither our love.
But darling, our love, was always meant to die.

*-For the words we never said, the love we kept behind
our screens (long distance love), and the ache that still
hums when I think of what we almost were.*

*

…………

Meri kavitaon ka aadhaar ho
Paas na ho kr bhi
Kambakht
Ishq ka bukhaar ho

………….

Love- the quiet kind

On lonely nights,
I built dreams
of fairy tale tomorrows
checklists of perfection
A Mr. Right made of smiles
and movie scenes.

Then you walked in
and I was electrified
Not by grand gestures
But by how you made space for me to breathe

You understood my chaos
made sense of my storms
and for the first time
I learned love could hum softly
doesn't need to be loud, but felt deeply.
It was calm.
It was kind.

A selenophile in love

Who knows what it feels like,
how I have spent the nights
In the wait of a new dawn,
At the same time waiting for twilight.

As the moon reminds me of you
And the stars tell the million reasons why
Some in your favour
while some twinkle just to make me cry.

But you do know the latter always lose the battle of lies
You know, the phases of the moon always bring in a
smile.

I know all this is just me talking to the skies
thinking they would respond in your voice.

The night sky shatters with the break of light
And I have to get up to live the new lies.
But at the end of the day.
I am a selenophile.
That's something I just cant deny.

From my diary, on a sleepless night when I missed someone who'd stopped missing me back and the moon was my only companion that night.

Too tired to feel

Sometimes,
I want to live inside a blanket.
Not under it- inside.
Tucked away in cotton silence,
where no one can look at me
like I've failed
at being okay.

I don't want eyes on me.
Not the world's
not even my own.

I want to unzip my chest
take out my heart
just for a while
to let it breathe
let it stop feeling so much.

And my brain?
It needs a massage.
The kind that goes deep.
past thoughts,
past noise,
into that place where peace

might still exist.

Because I'm tired
Not sleepy tired
Soul-tired

And I don't want answers.
I don't want fixing.

I just want to curl up into quiet and disappear,
for a little while.

-when getting up felt like a chore.

Still waiting for you

Last night you knocked on my door,
It was so dark I couldn't see.
But I felt it was you, even though you didn't say a thing.

I opened the door anyway,
because somehow, even in silence, you felt safe.

You walked in, drenched by the rain,
dressed in black,
still dashing as ever.

I hugged you,
it was the warmest place on earth,
even though you were dripping water everywhere.

The rain was weighing you down,
but you'd still carry me
if I didn't let go.
I wouldn't let go.

I'd stay here,
in this embrace,
for as long as I could.

I tell you, *this feels good.*
You tell me, *you are at the wrong place.*

A thunder cracks outside
and I wake up from my dream.

You are still a hundred miles away,
I am still waiting for you.

- for the nights when dreams bring them back just long enough to break your heart again.

*

....

Poetry aches so pretty.

....

*

....

Kabhi thi sard ye raatein
Tera aana Bahaara tha
Yahaan ke gham ke mausam mein
Tu hasne ka
Bahana tha.

....

*

....

I will just be the girl
you met at the bar one time
who you had amazing laughs with.
But by the end of the night
she was too afraid to give you her number.
Because she didn't want you to see her tears.

As at the end, people only remember the scars
Not the slitter hiding them.

-by a girl afraid of vulnerability.

....

Kabhi Kabhi

Kabhi-kabhi
kuch beete lamhe yaad aa jaate hain,
mere aaj se, ek pal chura le jaate hain.

jazbaaton se labalab bhare ye lamhe
ek pal mein muskurahat,
aur agle hi pal
aankho ko nam kr jaate hain.

*-on days you feel like you have moved on, but suddenly
you remember a moment, like you are living it all over
again, followed by the emptiness of their absence.*

*

....

She sat by the lake,
Watching the water shimmer as the sun went down.
These were the pictures she used to download from the internet,
trying to perfect each stroke of light, the reflection of the mountain, the sky crimson and pink.
But as she sat there, all she could think about was how much she wanted to share it with him.

-*when their absence make the loudest noise, in quiet moments.*

....

You still live in my routes

I run from silences
and walk away from quiet nights.
Play a song in the background
while I walk through my life.

Pretend your memories don't still linger,
and don't make my eyes heavy at night,
like they don't rush into my heart like electrolytes,
then drain me the next moment utterly dry.

I still take the longer route home,
Just to see if it still feels the same,
Like driving through the city on those nights,
like wind running through our hair
and us kissing under the moonlight.

Like the day you traced my cheek,
and said I deserved more than this.
That my heart was made for a kinder world
than the one we built in this heat.

Like I didn't know our world was bound to burn,
Like I didn't notice when you held back from falling too
deep.

You pretended I was the prize you were giving up
and I pretended I didn't know
your love was a disguise.

There's something familiar
about the ache of your lies
trinkets of truthful moments
I still revisit once in a while.

I don't want to miss you anymore,
but I still take the longer route home, every night.

*-For someone who never planned to stay, gave me
memories that still ache and I had mistaken the ache for
something like love.*

*

....

There is blankness in company
And noise in solitude.

....

Yaad hain vo baatein?

Aj shaam dhale uski yaad ne fir dastak di
Uski baatein chupte chupate dil ko jakad baithin
Mujhse dil ne kaha- yaad hain vo baatein?
Jab vo bin kahe, pyaar jatata tha
Tumhari khushi mei khud machal jaata tha
Tumhari ek shikan se bhi, vo ghabra jaata tha
Bin chuve tumhe apna mehsoos karata tha
Yaad hain so baatein tumhe?

Kaise khel hai khuda ke bhi,
Kisi shakhs se humein rubaro karaya,
Uski mohabbat mei humein mashroof karaya,
Aisi kismat likhi ki va bhi humse pyaar kare,
Par sirf chand lamhon ka saath qarar karaya,
Humari kismat mei mehez-yaadein likh aaya
mehez-baatein likh gaya.

Gulaab

Panno mein tera ansh
tere diye gulaab ki tarah
kaid reh gaya

khusboo toh nahi rahi
par laal nishaan reh gaya

-*when the pain they gave scars you, but you still keep
their memory intact ,like preserving a rose in a book.*

U-Turn

Firse chala mai uss sheher
jaha kabhi mera thikana tha,
Toofan se tooti, un sheeshon ne
dekha mera fasana tha.

Jis gali ki chandani ka
mai kabhi diwana tha,
unke andheron se aaj
rishta lagta purana tha.

Laga jin bazaaron mei lautne ka maqsad
sirf dil ko behlana tha,
vo asal mei uss gali se guzarne ka
ek bahana tha.

*-when you start falling for someone new , standing at
the edge of love again, but all it does is remind you of the
love you have lost.*

*

....

You're the low of my life that,
I want to visit all the time,
hoping you would turn into a high.
And putting myself through getting over you each time,
makes me realize,
I like punishing myself.

....

*

....

I am trying to mimic love
When my heart is tired-
Smiling at texts,
replying with warmth,
pretending I don't freeze
when someone says forever.

....

Am I in love, or in love with love?

He says *hello*
and my heart starts building temples.
Each syllable is a festival,
each glance, a sonnet
waiting to be written.

I take his filtered smiles
and turn them into love letters.
The way he says my name
feels like a confession he never made.

He once brushed my arm by accident;
I've replayed it enough
to make it look like fate.

When he laughs,
the rain becomes a symphony,
when e doesn't
the same clouds feel heavy again.

Its not his fault
he never promised me anything.
It's me:

the hopeless romantic,
the daydream architect,
the girl who turns casual greetings,
and empty silences
into poetry.

Because maybe I'm not in love with him.
Maybe I'm in love
with the story my heart tells,
every time someone says *hello,*
building castles out of thin air.

*

....

I've been high
On the broken love that I survived
You might think that's made me wise
Its only pretend
Just another lie.

....

Its self-preservation, My darling

You fall in love once,
he calls you a friend.
You fall in love twice,
he says you're not his type.

Around the third time,
you agree to play pretend.
You give him all your love,
and ask for nothing in return.

He says "I love your smile,
it makes everything bright."
You think it's a confession,
again, you read too much between the lines.

You makes a grand gesture
and gamble away your pride.
He walk away
as he never promised otherwise.

You're left with the mess he made,
and echoes of love misread.

Now your heart's such a mess,
it doesn't even know when it's hurt.
You cry at king gestures,
and laugh at cruel words.

You've built an armour around your heart
always falling for the wrong guy
has become your art.

So now you live in sweet delusion,
'cause truth feels like a cruel intrusion.
You chase the ones you know won't stay,
unreturned love is your only way.

And somewhere deep, your heart still hides,
afraid of love that truly abides.
You'll hand him maps of all your scars,
then lose yourself before you start.

It isn't foolishness.
Its self-preservation, my darling.
The only kind of love
you've ever been taught.

*-Sometimes self-preservation looks like falling in love
with the wrong person, because the right ones scare the
broken parts of you and delusion starts to feel like safety.*

The home I grew up in

The thing about growing up in a broken home
Is that your first example of love
is fights, followed by silences.
Its about your mom choosing other's comfort
and being left unrewarded, unacknowledged.

You are always at the mercy
Of you parents' moods
They could love you one moment for a joke you make,
and punish you for the same joke later that day.

You grow up in chaos,
In uncertainity of love.
The fickleness of it all.

And unlearning that kind of love is hard.
You've only seen love that's destined to die,
So you attract the same kind
the one where you are never chosen.

And by some twist of fate,
if you meet someone patient,
you flinch at their kindness,
and get uneasy with silence.

Because for you,
Love has never felt safe.

*-It took me years to realize, my first heartbreak didn't
come from a boy. It came from home.*

A funeral of you

A shot of poison
A bliss of sunshine
but one isn't enough
around the second time.

To feel that high again,
you empty a bottle of wine,
It stays a moment,
then you're back to chasing pints.

The silence starts to haunt you,
sitting in your company stings,
The chaos after every bottle
rearranges itself into sweet rhymes.

You look in the mirror,
don't recognize what you see
that girl with dream
has drowned in a deep sea.

To feel less guilty
you chug another down,
It becomes a cycle
you're stuck on the merry-go-round.

You lose yourself
your ambitions, your zeal.
everything hurts too much
unless you're in a sleep walking dream.

Alcohol became your companion
you thought it knew you best
No one really knows you
the real you is safely kept.

You dance a carefree ballet
in costumes carefully designed
by the ghosts of your insecurities,
to the best of needing to be liked.

You are running away from yourself,
trying to hide within you.
It's heartbreaking to witness
the quiet funeral of yourself.

-by a guilt-ridden addict, during a few sober moments.

*

....

Is it my father's detective eyes
or my mother's biased lens
that has made my vision of myself?

....

*

....

I've spent so long learning to shrink
to take up space,
that even while writing these poems
I flinch, afraid someone will say,
I'm making too much of a noise with my pen.

....

When summer was kind

There was a time
when summer was kind
it smelled of mangoes
and tangy-spicy-lime.

That backyard at my grandma's,
where red guava trees would bloom,
we built paper planes and dreams
that never left the room.

Love then was laughter,
and joy meant new toys,
a doll in my lap,
a world full of noise.

Fireflies danced with us,
in evenings soft and slow,
we made friends out of shadows,
and hearts out of glow.

But growing up's been harder
than I thought it would be
love now feels heavier,
and joy's not as free.

Now summers taste different
the mangoes less sweet, the days less wide.
I still fold paper sometimes,
but the planes don't fly that high.

Maybe kindness was simpler then,
and love was always in view
when the world was just a backyard,
and joy was something we knew.

*- from the summer I missed my my nani and her garden
way too much. I love you always amma.*

*

....

I felt sane when I had lost my mind,
Thinking you still cared.
Now that you're really gone,
It feels like a void.
But I am more aware,

....

Torn

I am torn between
the want to be loved
and the promise to love myself enough.

The comfort of someone's arms,
the familiarity in another heartbeat,
the longing to belong,
and craving to be seen.

But the feminist in me,
snaps at the idea of modern love,
because its always been a game
with rules that *they* set.

The woman I am today
was built by pain,
from each heartbreak,
and broken promises she gained.

She learned to turn the hurt
into poetry that spoke,
taught herself to love kindly,
even when her faith almost broke.

How am I supposed to shrink
Into the mould of fantasy
that fits every man's dream.
And how am I supposed to stay mute
when I am just learning to be fluent
to speak my truth?

I would love to make a home,
that is warm and sweet,
but I have seen my mother disappear,
into the very walls she had lovingly built.

So I flinch and scream,
at the idea of losing myself,
and everything that I have built.

They want us to be pretty,
of a specific kind
to be smart but not forget,
that there is a line, that *they* can set.
To shine bright and have dreams,
but not enough to steal the spotlight.

A housekeeper with spark and drive,
who's taught to shrink,
yet forced to thrive.

-written on a day I realized I'm done performing softness for survival.

Doll

They say, *Be strong, Don't cry,*
Don't be fragile, like a doll
that could break.

But where were they
when I held my own hand,
and taught myself to breathe,
through the flood of tears all night?

They say, *Be stoic,*
the world will hurt you,
it will walk all over you
if you don't abide to their rules.

But this world has never been kind,
never been fair.

Keep it in,
don't show you hurt,
As if being human
were a crime.

Yet in this world of staged smile,
and counterfeit love,

I still write poems
that make someone believe again,
So, how am I wrong
and the world considered right?

Because faith in love,
and the stubborn hope inn goodness,
that's not my weakness.
Its the only way I'm alive.

-from the night I refused to harden my heart.

Romanticising Rain

The sound of rain
brings so many memories.

It reminds me of the kid
who jumped on puddles
and made paper boats that could dream.

Of flowers that bloom
and make the world bright,
the smell of jasmine —
so soothing, yet wild inside.

It reminds me of the day
when we first met,
you gave your coat to the dogs,
and my heart —
in your pocket you kept.

The day you said *"I love you,"*
and it was raining again,
the sky shimmered with lightning
like it was celebrating our names.

I asked if it'd last forever,

and you said *"yes."*
But it was an empty promise,
a broken thread.

It reminds me of the nights
I spent crying in bed —
rain, my only companion,
when my heart had bled.

But now, it's different —
in this rented place I call home,
I sip my tea on the balcony,
and no longer feel alone.

The rain still sings its music,
but the tune has changed its tone —
it makes my tea taste sweeter,
and reminds me I've grown.

-Growing up, I've always romanticised the rain — like a
lover girl who never stopped believing in magic. It's
soothed me, excited me, and given me butterflies. This
one's from the romantic in me.

Kaisi paheli hai tu zindagi

Kaisi paheli hai tu zindagi
Pehle Khushiyon se mujhe milati hai
Mujhe kehti hai –
Pagli, haq hai tera,
Thoda hass le,
Teri-meri katti thi
Ab mujhe kasle
Naraaz mai bhi toh chal rahi thi tujhse
Ab dosti karle.

Par jab mai tujhe thamoon
Tu gainron si ho jaati hai
Choti-choti baton pe mujhe rulati hai.

Pehle baarish se phoolon ko rang chadhati hai
Fir sirf toofaano ki dhool udati hai

Har bar tu mujhe muskurana sikhati hai
Par har bar khona bhi sikhati hai

Rukti nahi tu mere liye
Bas apni dhun mei
thirakti
Aage badh jaati hai

Jitna bhi mai tujhe rokun
Tu vo khushiyan bhi saath le jaati hai

Kaisi paheli hai tu zindagi
Kyu mujhe itna satati hai?

-From the day I realised my life has been a roller coaster of ups and downs but somehow I am still grateful for the few good moments.

*

....

You're not an outcast
You're extra ordinary.

....

Parul

There's a girl who walks like quiet rain,
Soft where the world is hard,
She builds her peace from jasmine plants,
And heartbreak turned into art.

She's lived a thousand years by 28,
With a laugh that hides the ache,
She's made herself from scattered stars,
Each bruise, each burn, each break.

She wears her dresses like armor now,
Lipstick like a blade,
Still, she dreams of beaches and soft guitars,
Of love that doesn't fade.

She is not naive, don't say it so,
She hopes—despite the fall.
Hope, my darling, is not weakness,
It's the bravest thing of all.

-A self portrait after finally beginning to fall in love with myself. Embracing my quirks and calling it romantic

*

....

You are not the punch-line,

You are the plot twist, my darling.

....

*

....

I am living the truth of my heart,

I am slowly and surely

Coming to a new start.

....

What love finally looks like

For the longest time,
love for me was a dream.
It was dipped in fantasy,
and proposals on big screens.

The belief that "happily ever after"
still exists—
came from my hero, who said
unrequited love
was the most *beautiful* thing.

Then I chased those stories,
where the prince always chooses
the clueless queen—
he's the knight in shining armour
who brings closure for his queen.

Through each broken pinky promise,
I lost a piece of me,
gambling away my childhood dreams,
of stories I wished to live.

It wasn't all bad—
some heartbreaks were meant to teach

that love doesn't always come in fireworks,
it's also felt in silence,
and could be sweet.

It's measured in actions,
not in repeated quotes, that sound too deep.

Love isn't always romantic.
It could live in a conversation with your best friend,
a cup of tea with your mother,
a carefully made dish by your amma,
or that quiet comfort from your father.

After getting destroyed
in the hurricane of love each time,
I've finally learned—
love isn't demanding,
doesn't need to drain you dry.

Love is real when you love yourself,
when it inspires you
to bring light into others' lives.

-For the girl who spent years chasing love outside

herself, only to find it blooming quietly within.

*

....

If my words found your ache,
then maybe our hearts
were meant to meet here.

....

Thank you for listening

....